A Pet's Life

Cats

Anita Ganeri

Heinemann
LIBRARY

www.heinemann.co.uk/library

Visit our website to find out more information about **Heinemann Library** books.

To order:

☎ Phone 44 (0) 1865 888066

▤ Send a fax to 44 (0) 1865 314091

▢ Visit the Heinemann Bookshop at www.heinemann.co.uk/library to browse our catalogue and order online.

First published in Great Britain by Heinemann Library, Halley Court, Jordan Hill, Oxford OX2 8EJ, part of Harcourt Education. Heinemann is a registered trademark of Harcourt Education Ltd.

Editorial: Jilly Attwood and Claire Throp
Design: Richard Parker and Tinstar Design Limited (www.tinstar.co.uk)
Picture Research: Rosie Garai
Production: Séverine Ribierre

Originated by Dot Gradations
Printed and bound in China by South China Printing Company

ISBN 0 431 17762 7   (hardback)
07 06 05 04 03
10 9 8 7 6 5 4 3 2 1

ISBN 0 431 17780 5   (paperback)
07 06 05 04 03
10 9 8 7 6 5 4 3 2 1

British Library Cataloguing in Publication Data

Ganeri, Anita
    Cats – (A Pet's Life)
    636.8
A full catalogue record for this book is available from the British Library.

Acknowledgements

The publishers would like to thank the following for permission to reproduce photographs: Ardea **pp. 4, 20, 21** (John Daniels); Corbis/Reflections Photolibrary **p. 23** (Jennie Woodstock); Corbis **p. 27** (Tom Stewart); Dave Bradford **pp. 12, 18**; DK Images **p. 16**; RSPCA **pp. 10, 25, 26** (Angela Hampton); Super Stock **p. 8**; Tudor Photography **pp. 9, 14, 19**; Warren Photographic **p. 22**; Warren Photographic **pp. 5, 6, 7, 11, 13, 15, 17, 24** (Jane Burton)

Cover photograph reproduced with permission of Bruce Coleman/Werner Layer.

The publishers would like to thank Pippa Bush of the RSPCA for her assistance in the preparation of this book.

Every effort has been made to contact copyright holders of any material reproduced in this book. Any omissions will be rectified in subsequent printings if notice is given to the publishers.

RSPCA Trading Limited (which pays all its taxable profits to the RSPCA, Registered Charity No. 219099) receives a royalty for every copy of this book sold by Heinemann Library. Details of the royalties payable to RSPCA Trading Limited can be obtained by writing to the Publisher, Heinemann Library, Halley Court, Jordan Hill, Oxford, OX2 8EJ. For the purposes of the Charities Act 1992 no further seller of this book shall be deemed to be a commercial participator with the RSPCA. RSPCA name and logo are trademarks of the RSPCA used by Heinemann Library under licence from RSPCA Trading Ltd.

Contents

Any words appearing in the text in bold, **like this**, are explained in the Glossary.

What is a cat?

Cats are very popular pets. There are many kinds of pet cats. Cats can be big or small. Cats can have long or short hair.

This cat is called a **Persian cat**.

Sharp, pointed teeth for holding food.

Long tail for balance.

Ears for sharp hearing.

Eyes for seeing well in dim light.

Whiskers for feeling in the dark.

Rough tongue for grooming.

Fur coat for warmth.

Claws for climbing and scratching.

Here you can see the different parts of a cat's body and what each part is used for.

Cat babies

Baby cats are called kittens. A new-born kitten is small and helpless. Its mother licks it to keep it clean. The kitten opens its eyes when it is 5–10 days old.

New-born kittens feed on their mother's milk.

Kittens must be about eight weeks old
before they can leave their mother.
Then they are ready to be chosen as pets.

Kittens love to play with
their brothers and sisters.

Your pet cat

Looking after a cat is fun but it also takes lots of time. You need to look after your cat every day, for the whole of its life.

If you look after your cat, it will quickly become your best friend.

If you go on holiday, ask a friend or neighbour to look after your cat. Otherwise you can put your cat in a **cattery**.

Make a list of what your friend needs to do.

Choosing your cat

The best place to find a cat or kitten is an **animal shelter**. They are always looking for good homes for cats of all kinds and ages.

You might decide to get an adult cat instead of a kitten.

Pick a cat or kitten with bright eyes and a clean nose. Check that its coat is shiny and that its bottom is dry and clean.

Look for a friendly, lively kitten that likes to play.

Things to get ready

Before you bring your new pet home, you should get everything ready. Your cat will need a cosy basket or bed to sleep in.

Put your cat's bed in a clean, quiet place.

Your cat will also need a plastic **litter tray** where it can go to the toilet. You can buy one from a pet shop.

Clean the litter tray every day. Don't forget to wash your hands afterwards.

Welcome home

You can carry your cat home in a special carrying box made from wire or plastic. Line the box with newspaper and a warm blanket or towel.

A carrying box is also useful for taking your cat to the vet.

For a few days, leave your new pet in one room to settle in quietly. Then you can let it explore the whole house.

If you have another cat or a dog, let your new pet get to know it slowly.

Feeding time

You can feed your cat on dry or tinned food. Adult cats need two meals a day. Kittens should have three to four smaller meals.

Kittens should have special kitten food to help them grow.

Make sure that your cat always has clean water to drink. It is not a good idea to give your cat milk. It might make it ill.

Wash your cat's food and water bowls every day.

Training your cat

Kittens have to be toilet-trained. Start by lifting your kitten gently into its **litter tray**. Do this often until it learns to use the tray.

Use both hands to pick your cat up so that you support its weight.

Most cats like to go outside. Fit a **cat-flap**
into your door. At first, you can prop it
open to let your cat go in and out.

Your cat will quickly learn
to nudge the cat-flap
open with its head.

Playing with your cat

Kittens love to play. You can buy cat toys from a pet shop. But cardboard tubes, cotton reels and paper bags also make good toys.

Playing helps your kitten to learn how to hunt.

Your cat has to scratch with its claws to keep them sharp. Outside, cats can scratch trees. But a scratching post is best indoors.

A scratching post is covered in carpet or rope

Growing up

Kittens grow up very quickly. By the time they are a year old, they are adult cats. Male cats usually grow bigger than female cats.

The cat on the left is male. You can see that he is bigger than the female.

There are lots of unwanted cats and kittens. So it is best to have your kitten or cat **neutered** to stop it having babies. Ask your vet about this.

As it gets older, your pet will still like to play.

A healthy cat

You need to look after your cat to make sure that it stays healthy. If you are worried about your cat, take it to a vet.

If your cat stops eating or drinking, it may be unwell.

When you get a new cat, take it to the vet for a check-up. The vet will give your cat injections to stop it catching nasty **diseases**.

Your cat will need a check-up once a year.

Old age

Cats can live for a long time, usually for about 12–16 years. As your cat gets older, it might need special care.

As it gets older, your cat will want to sleep more.

It can be very upsetting when your pet dies. Try not to be too sad. Just remember all the happy times that you shared.

Caring for your cat will help you learn how to treat animals properly.

Useful tips

- If your cat goes outside, it should wear a collar and tag with your name and address on it. Choose a collar that will snap open if it gets caught on the branch of a tree.

- Cats are very clean and **groom** themselves. But you need to brush long-haired cats every day to stop them swallowing too much fur and getting **fur balls**.

- Treat your cat regularly with medicines to stop it getting fleas and worms. Ask your vet what you should do.

- Look at the label on the cat food to find out how much to give to your cat. Don't give your cat too much to eat.

- Plant some **catmint** in your garden. Cats love to roll in it!

Fact file

- Cats were first kept as pets about 4000 years ago. They were used to catch mice and rats.

- In Ancient Egypt, cats were popular pets. When they died, they were made into mummies.

- Cats can sleep for 16–18 hours a day.

- The oldest pet cat known was a tabby (a cat with a stripey coat) called Ma. It died in 1957, at the age of 34.

- Your pet cat's wild relations include lions, tigers, leopards and cheetahs.

- The Ragdoll cat gets its name because it goes floppy when it is picked up.

Glossary

animal shelter a place where lost or unwanted animals are looked after and found new homes

cat-flap a see-through flap which you fit in a door to let your cat go in and out

catmint a strong-smelling plant that most cats love. The dried leaves are called catnip.

cattery a place where you can leave your cat when you go on holiday

diseases illnesses

fur balls balls of fur in a cat's tummy. The cat has to be sick to get rid of them.

groom brush your cat. Cats also groom themselves using their rough tongues.

litter tray a box where a cat can go to the toilet. It is filled with special gravel called litter.

neutered when a cat has an operation so that it cannot have any babies

Persian cat cat with a very fluffy coat

More information

Books to read

First Pets: Cats and Kittens, K. Starke (Usborne Publishing, 1999)

How to Look After Your Pet: Kitten, Mark Evans (Dorling Kindersley, 1992)

The Official RSPCA Pet Guide: Care for your Cat (HarperCollins, 1990)

The Official RSPCA Pet Guide: Care for your Kitten (HarperCollins, 1990)

Websites

www.rspca.org.uk
   The website of The Royal Society for the Prevention of Cruelty to Animals in Britain.

www.pethealthcare.co.uk
   Information about keeping and caring for pets.

www.petnet.au.com
   Information about being a good pet owner.

Index

Titles in the *A Pet's Life* series include:

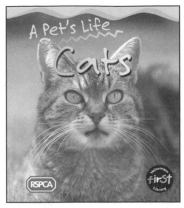

Hardback   0 431 17762 7

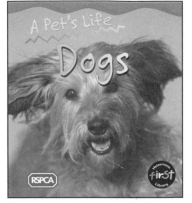

Hardback   0 431 17764 3

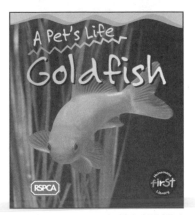

Hardback   0 431 17765 1

Hardback   0 431 17761 9

Hardback   0 431 17763 5

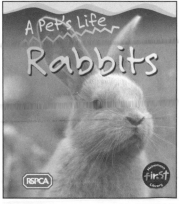

Hardback   0 431 17760 0

Find out about the other titles in this series on our website www.heinemann.co.uk/library